Could UFO's Be Real?

by Larry Koss,
Editorial Director

**Published By
Capstone Press, Inc.
Mankato, Minnesota USA**

Distributed By
ℂℙ CHILDRENS PRESS®
CHICAGO

CIP
LIBRARY OF CONGRESS CATALOGING IN PUBLICATION DATA

Could UFOS be real / Larry Koss, project editor.
p. cm.
Summary: Examines sightings, studies, and projects related to unidentified flying objects and discusses the search for life in space.

ISBN 1-56065-093-1:
1. Unidentified flying objects --Juvenile literature.   2. Unidentified flying objects--Research--Juvenile literature.
[1. Unidentified flying objects.] I. Koss, Larry.
TL236.S735   1989
629.222--dc20
                                                CIP
                                                AC

PHOTO CREDITS

Larry Koss: page 4
Antonioa Huneeus: pages 9, 16, 25, 29, 36, 41, 45, 48

CAPSTONE PRESS
Box 669, Mankato, MN 56001

Contents

COULD UFO'S BE REAL?

Introduction by Richard Hall

Unexplained things have been seen in the sky for *thousands* of years.

In Egypt about 1500 B.C., a Pharaoh and his people saw "circles of fire" in the air.

Pilgrim John Winthrop wrote about a UFO seen in 1638. He reported that a glowing object swooped down on three men in a boat near Boston harbor at night. It scared them. They felt something pulling them against the tide. Other people on shore saw the object, too. They said it shot out flames and sparks. The sighting lasted for about 20 minutes.

There are UFO reports from England, France, Italy and Spain. There are reports from India, South Africa, Australia, Argentina, and Brazil. Some of the India and Australia reports are very, very old. Think of it. UFOs were reported long before the Wright brothers flew their first airplane.

The most important fact about these worldwide sightings is that they show *patterns*. People in places thousands of miles apart describe the same kind of UFOs. They also describe the same kinds of things that UFOs *do*.

On January 21, 1977, a glowing object flew over two men in a boat at night in Louisiana. They felt the boat being pulled backward. The boat engine *pushed*, but the UFO *pulled* just as hard. The engine continued to run, but the boat could not move in the water. An oil company guard on shore also saw the UFO. This sighting was very similar to the one in 1638, 300 years earlier.

Until they are investigated, UFO sightings are only stories. They don't prove anything. People report all kinds of mysteries which may or may not be real. In fact, most UFOs turn out to have simple explanations. They have to be carefully investigated first. If an explanation is found, they become IFOs. IFOs are *Identified* Flying Objects!

There is a reason why there are so many UFO "false alarms." A lot of people don't look at the sky very often. They do not know about stars, planets, or meteors. They haven't paid attention to how airplanes look at night.

Sometimes haze or moving clouds pass in front of bright stars or planets. Then the stars or planets can look like they are moving. Even the moon can look funny when partly hidden by dark clouds. Aircraft strobe lights flash brightly so other planes will see them. But if you don't know what they are, you will just notice bright white flashes and many think they are UFOs.

Advertising planes that carry brightly lit messages have led to UFO reports. So has the Goodyear blimp.

When UFO reports are in the news, many people go outside to try to see one for themselves. If they are not used to looking at the sky, they may see all kinds of strange things. They may be fooled by ordinary things that are not UFOs at all.

For example, most people think of meteors as "shooting stars." Meteors look like a small dot of light darting across the sky for about one second before burning out. Few people know about "fireball" meteors.

Fireball meteors look very large. Witnesses say they can look almost as big as the moon. They can look like an airplane on fire, about to crash into the next field. But they really may be hundreds of miles away. Many fireballs have a long glowing trail. They can last as long as 15 to 20 seconds before burning out.

Large fireballs may break up in the earth's atmosphere. They can make a loud rumbling noise that sounds like a train. If a fireball or any meteor hits the earth it becomes a meteo*rite*. Years ago, people thought that it was impossible that stones could "fall from heaven." But when you see meteorites in a science museum, you will see that it is true. Meteorites are partly melted pieces of stone or metal which really did "fall from heaven!" Astronomers think they may be little pieces of "leftovers" from when the solar system was formed.

UFO investigators must know about astronomy, aviation, natural science, and many other subjects. They must be able to tell a UFO from an IFO. After they study everything the UFO witnesses said, there is more to do. Evidence, such as broken tree branches, or burned grass, must be studied. There may be photographs or radar tracks to look at. A good UFO investigator is a good detective. Most times he or she will find that the witness saw an IFO. But some sightings will turn out to be true UFOs.

One of the many space shots of possible UFOs taken by NASA Astronauts during Gemini 12 Mission in November, 1966, officially explained as probable debris from the capsule.

UFO SIGHTINGS

By Bruce Maccabee, Ph.D.

Modern UFO sightings began early in 1947. In January a British military airplane chased an unidentified object which it could not catch. In April, weathermen and others saw strange, shiny round objects flying through the sky. In May the witnesses included pilots and railroad workers. In early June, as the sightings started to increase, about two dozen sightings were made by people including pilots.

All of these witnesses were puzzled. They had no idea what they had seen. They knew that many scientific and aviation discoveries had come out of World War II. Maybe they were seeing some new type of aircraft.

On June 24, 1947, Kenneth Arnold was flying his small plane near the town of Mineral, in Washington State. He was a pilot and business-man with many years of flying experience. At about 3:00 p.m. he saw bright flashes of light. Quickly he looked around to see if there was another airplane nearby reflecting the bright sunlight.

Instead of another airplane, he saw a number of objects flying in a row southward past Mt. Rainier. They were lower than the mountaintop and looked dark against the snowy slopes of this ancient volcano. Arnold was surprised because they were not shaped like airplanes. They looked more like half-circles. He could not see any engines or tails on them.

He could see that they were about 20 miles away from him as they began flying in and out of the mountain peaks south of Mt. Rainier. They rocked back and forth as they moved through the mountains. As they rocked or wobbled back and forth, the bright sunlight flashed off them like a mirror.

Arnold thought he was looking at some new type of jet airplane, and he wondered how fast they were traveling. He timed them, using the dashboard clock on his airplane, as they flew from Mt. Rainier to Mt. Adams about 47 miles to the south. The UFOs crossed that space of sky in 102 seconds (1.7 minutes). This figured out to be a speed of about 1600 m.p.h., more than twice the speed of sound. This was several months before test pilot Chuck Yeager set a speed record by flying just above the speed of sound, 746 m.p.h.

Arnold was amazed. He did not know at the time that Fred Johnson, a prospector (searching the area for valuable minerals) was working near Mt. Adams and saw the objects fly by. When Arnold landed in Yakima he told some friends that he had seen some new type of military aircraft. Then he flew on to Pendleton, Oregon.

During this flight some newspaper reporters learned about his sighting, and they were waiting for him when he landed. He carefully described what he had seen, how he had timed the speed, and his conclusion that he had seen a new type of military aircraft.

The reporters were impressed. Arnold's story was published in newspapers across the country. Some unknown headline writer used Arnold's description of how the objects flew – like a saucer skipping across the water – and the term *flying saucer* was born. It was only many years later that they began to be called Unidentified Flying Objects or UFOs.

Various scientists or experts tried to explain Arnold's sighting. One of them, Dr. Donald Menzel, a director of Harvard College Observatory, gave five different explanations. He wrote three books in which he claimed to explain UFO sightings. His "explanations" of the Arnold sighting included blowing clouds of snow, rapidly moving clouds, reflections of sunlight from layers of the atmosphere, mirages of the mountaintops, and water droplets on the windshield of Arnold's plane.

A few days after Arnold's sighting was reported in the newspapers, people all over the U.S. began to report seeing similar objects in the sky. The reports continued through July of 1947. About 1,000 sightings were made at this time. About 800 of them were reported in local newspapers.

All kinds of people reported sightings. The most important witnesses were military men and pilots. They knew what normal aircraft were like. On July 8 at Muroc Air Force Base (now called

Edwards Air Force Base) and Rogers Dry Lake in California, there was a very important series of sightings. Military men on the bases saw odd-shaped, shiny objects flying over the area at high speed. The Air Force (a branch of the Army at that time) was interested in these sightings. Rogers Dry Lake in recent years has been used as a landing field for the NASA Space Shuttle.

On July 7, 1947, a man in Phoenix, Arizona, took the first clear photographs of a UFO. The object had a round, curved front and a concave rear. Overall it was shaped like a fat crescent. This was similar to what Arnold had seen.

A much more important case happened a day or so earlier in Roswell, New Mexico. A farmer called the Roswell Air Base to say that he had found wreckage of some highly unusual object on his land. A special team of military men headed by Major Jesse Marcel went to the location of the crash. They took all of the wreckage for the Air Force to study.

On July 8 the Roswell newspaper published a story which said that the Air Force had found a "flying saucer." That night the Air Force said the "saucer" was only a crashed weather balloon. A special Air Force message to the FBI shows that the unusual material was shipped to Wright Field (now Wright-Patterson AFB) in Dayton, Ohio, for analysis.

The 1947 sightings reached a peak in July, then slowed down. Scientists and other "experts" were asked for their opinions by reporters. They suggested *many different* explanations for the sightings. Many thought that the witnesses had not recognized natural events related to meteorology (weather) or astronomy. One science writer said people were seeing *motes* in their eyes (specks that seem to float in your eye when you move it).

The Air Force was serious about the sightings and continued to investigate them. Also, the sightings continued but at a much lower rate.

Taken by the official photographer for the Coast
Guard Air Station in Salem, Mass. on July 17, 1952.

The 1950's:
Sightings, Investigations, and the Extraterrestrial Hypothesis

In January 1950 Major Donald Keyhoe, a retired Marine Corps pilot who had become a well-known writer, had an article about UFOs in TRUE magazine. He claimed that "inside sources" of Air Force information had led him to believe that the flying saucers were real. (The title of his article was "Flying Saucers Are Real.") His sources also told him that the Air Force was keeping evidence secret. In his article he suggested that the sightings could be explained by the "extraterrestrial hypothesis" (the idea that some UFO sightings were caused by spaceships from outside the Earth).

Mr. Keyhoe's article stirred up a lot of interest in UFOs. It suggested that either "flying saucers" or UFOs were from outer space, or the people who reported them were badly fooled, or hoaxers. His article also raised the question: How much does the Air Force know about UFOs that it has not told the public?

Two of the most famous pictures and one of the most famous movies also were taken in 1950. On May 11, a farmer and his wife near McMinnville, Oregon, saw and photographed a round, flat (disc-like or circular) UFO. On August 15 a man in Great Falls, Montana, took a movie of two UFOs.

In the fall of 1951 a series of sightings took place at Fort Monmouth, New Jersey. An Air Force pilot saw and chased a large shiny disc while an Army Signal Corps radar detected a fast-moving object. These sightings attracted the attention of an Air Force general. He ordered the UFO project to increase and improve its study of UFOs.

Early in 1951, a scientific consulting group that does secret military research, the Battelle Memorial Institute, carried out a statistical study of UFO sightings. They analyzed about 3,200 sightings collected by the Air Force between 1947 and the end of 1952. Their work was almost finished in 1953, but the final report was not published until 1955. It was called *Project Blue Book Special Report No. 14.*

During the summer of 1952, the largest number of sightings over the U.S. took place. From June through August Project Blue Book received about 1,000 sightings. This was more than had been received by the Air Force in any single *year* up until then. Sightings over Washington, D.C. in July made front page headlines all over the country. UFOs were tracked on radar and chased by Air Force fighter planes around Washington. These sightings caused the Central Intelligence Agency (CIA) to start its own investigation to see if UFOs were a threat to the U.S.

On July 1 a very important movie of UFOs was taken by Navy photographer Delbert Newhouse near Tremonton, Utah. After many hours of photographic analysis by the Navy, the images (bright, round objects) remained unexplained. The UFOs were circular and shiny when he first saw them. By the time he started filming them they were too far away for the camera to pick up details. Military and civilian intelligence agencies quickly learned about the movie. An FBI agent working with the Air Force reported to FBI headquarters that "...some military officials are seriously considering the possibility of interplanetary ships."

The Battelle said that the Air Force received 2,018 sightings in 1951. Of these, 465 (or 23%) were listed as unexplained.

Late in 1952 the CIA decided to form a special committee of scientists to study UFO sightings and find out if they were any kind of threat to the U.S. This was before the Battelle study was even finished. The special committee of scientists was called the Robertson panel because its chairman was Dr. H. P. Robertson. It included several well-known scientists and a Nobel Prize winner.

The committee met in January 1953 to analyze UFO sightings presented to them by the Project Blue Book staff. Blue Book had concluded that about 20% of the sightings could not be explained. The Robertson panel disagreed. They concluded that all sightings could be explained. They recommended several things for Project Blue Book to do. Most of all, that Project Blue Book should explain the sightings and tell the public about all the ordinary things seen in the sky that they are mistaking for UFOs. They felt that public education would stop people from reporting IFOs (Identified Flying Objects) as UFOs.

The sudden increase of UFO sightings in 1952 caused a reaction from scientists. They suggested many different explanations for why people would report things as flying saucers. One scientist took the lead in explaining UFO sightings. That was Dr. Donald Menzel, director of Harvard College Observatory. He suggested that natural events in the atmosphere caused many sightings. The average person just didn't know about haloes around the sun and unusual mirages caused by weather conditions.

Dr. Menzel's first book *Flying Saucers* (Harvard University Press, Cambridge, Mass.) was published in 1953. In this book he said that all UFO sightings that didn't have other obvious explanations were caused by unusual natural events in the atmosphere. Many scientists who were too busy to study UFO reports themselves thought that Menzel had taken care of the problem. There was no reason to believe UFOs were anything important.

In May 1955 the Battelle report was published. Only a summary of it was given to the news media. Just the few people who got copies of the whole report were able to study the facts. The summary said that the chances were "very small or zero" that any of the sightings were of new flying technology (actual craft or machine). It said that since 1953 the Air Force had improved its investigation and analysis of UFO sightings. As a result they had been able to reduce the percentage of unexplained cases to 9% during 1953 and 1954, and to only 3% during the first half of 1955.

The summary also said that the Air Force had received a total of 4,834 sightings between 1947 and 1954. Of these, 854 were received during 1953 and 1954.

In later years the Air Force used the summary to back up its claim that UFOs were not a threat and there was no evidence that any of them were spaceships. When the complete report finally was released to the public in 1976, we learned that several important facts were left out of the summary. The summary did not say that almost

22% of the sightings between 1947 and 1952 were left unexplained. Nor did it say that the largest number of unexplained sightings happened in 1952 while the Battelle study was being made.

The summary did not say that when sightings were divided up by how good or poor the witnesses and information were 33% of the "excellent" sightings could not be explained.

The summary did not mention that UFO sightings were being made all over the world. It did not mention that the Battelle analysis had pointed out 20 unexplained sightings "...that were observed in such a way that they should have been recognized easily if they had been familiar objects."

Finally, the summary did not mention the "twelve good unknowns" singled out by Battelle and described individually. One of these was a round, flat object seen by employees of an aeronautical laboratory and observed through binoculars. They said it approached, hovered, rotated like a top, then took off with the speed of a jet aircraft. All this time it made no sound.

Everyone who studied UFO sightings in the 1950s discovered that UFO sightings were not limited to the U.S. The general public was not aware of this because the news media typically did not report sightings in other countries. However, Air Force intelligence services were aware of it. A table of statistics buried in the back of the summary showed the following breakdown of sightings for 1943-1952:

	Sightings	Unexplained
North America (Including Alaska and Hawaii)	2,969	638 (21%)
Canada alone	81	22 (27%)
South America	10	1 (10%)
Europe	80	14 (18%)
Asia	115	32 (28%)
Africa	25	4 (16%)

This table shows that people on most of the major continents had reported UFO sightings by 1952.

Taken in Barra da Tijuca, a suburb of Rio de Janeiro, Brazil in May 7, 1952.

In 1954, sightings picked up again, in France, Spain, and Italy. Civilian UFO groups were started in these countries too.

A Royal Canadian Air Force pilot, Robert Childerhose, saw and photographed a UFO in 1955 while flying in a squadron of four Sabre Jets over Manitoba, Canada.

In 1957 a UFO was photographed by someone on board a Brazilian naval research ship. The UFO was round with a ring around the center (like the planet Saturn). Naval officers on board saw the UFO, watched the photographer take the pictures, and saw the results when the film was developed. They said that the photographs showed exactly what they had seen.

October 1957 was the time of the first UFO "abduction" report. An abduction is when a person says that he or she was taken on board a UFO (some kind of craft) and examined by alien beings while on board. A Brazilian farmer named Antonio Villas Boas, 23 years old, said this happened to him on October 15, 1957, while he was alone plowing a field after midnight.

After 1957 the sightings dropped off again. Project Blue Book received 627 reports in 1958 and 390 in 1959. The total number of unexplained cases at the end of 1959 was 851. This was about 10% of the total sightings.

In 1961 the House Committee on Science and Astronautics of the Congress took an interest in UFOs. They asked the Air Force questions. But the Air Force convinced the Committee that it was doing everything it could to investigate UFO sightings. Congress took no further action at that time.

In 1964 a report had an important impact on UFO history. On April 24, police officer Lonnie Zamora in Socorro, New Mexico, was chasing a speeder in the afternoon. When he heard what he thought was an explosion, he broke off the chase. He went to investigate the explosion and found an egg-shaped object on the ground. Standing next to it were two small people. The people looked at Zamora and seemed to be surprised. They disappeared into the object which then took off and flew away.

Local and State Police were called to the scene. They found markings on the ground where the UFO had landed. Apparently it was a real craft. An FBI agent and Army and Air Force investigators went to the landing site. They talked with Zamora, measured the markings and wrote reports. The case was widely reported in the news. It was very believable and convinced a lot of people that UFOs were real after all.

Two important people who were impressed by the Socorro report were Major Hector Quintanilla, director of Project Blue Book and

Dr. J. Allen Hynek, Air Force scientific consultant.

Several years later Major Quintanilla wrote in an intelligence agency publication that it was the most puzzling case he had ever received. He could not explain it. Dr. Hynek later said that it was this case that finally convinced him UFOs deserved very serious study. It appeared to be an unexplainable flying craft.

UFO landing tracks in Socorro, New Mexico on April 24, 1964.

In 1965 UFO sightings began to increase not only in the U.S., but also in such countries as Australia, Chile, and Argentina. During the late summer the Air Force recorded about 500 of the nearly 900 cases for the whole year. A series of sightings took place at scientific stations in Antarctica in June and July. Witnesses included military men from Chile, Argentina, and England. Argentina and Chile both made public statements about the sightings and they were reported in newspapers.

A special panel of scientists met in February 1966 and reviewed the methods, resources and findings of Project Blue Book. They suggested that the Air Force give a contract to one or more colleges to study UFOs. The colleges would provide teams of experts to investigate sightings quickly and thoroughly.

While the Air Force inner circles were struggling with the question of what to do about UFOs, a new outbreak of sightings increased public demand for action. During the night of March 14, 1966 citizens and police officers near Ann Arbor, Michigan, were astounded by strangely lighted objects that put on an aerial display. Near Dexter, Michigan, two officers saw four discs flying in a line. They reported that the objects could move very quickly and make very sharp turns.

On the night of March 20, near Dexter, Michigan, a farmer and his son saw a bright object land in a swampy area. They called the police, and two officers came to investigate. They all saw an object with flashing red, white and blue lights rise up, hover for a few minutes, and then streak away. Similar objects were seen by others, and police tried to chase some of them.

The climax came on the night of March 21 near a college in Hillsdale, Michigan. There were nearly 100 witnesses including a dormitory full of students, a college Dean, a Civil Defense Director, and several police officers. A glowing, football-shaped UFO hovered and moved around in a swampy area for several hours. Finally it moved away over a wooded area and disappeared. An increase in radioactivity was measured in the area where the UFO had been hovering.

Major national news media including TV networks now swarmed into Michigan. The Air Force was under pressure to find explanations. Major Quintanilla asked Dr. Hynek, as scientific consultant, to go to Hillsdale and investigate personally. Dr. Hynek only had a day or two before he was told to present his explanation of what was being seen to newsmen in a press conference on March 25.

Dr. Hynek later admitted that he did not have an explanation. In answer to questions by newsmen he pointed out that the March 20 and 21 sightings had happened over swampy areas. He suggested that "very likely" the sightings were "swamp gas" being released during spring thaw. (Swamp or marsh gas from decaying vegetation can ignite and glow a faint blue, but it flickers and goes out quickly and never rises high off the ground.) He made no comments about the other sightings away from swampy areas.

The witnesses were angry about this attempted explanation. They had seen large discs and football shaped objects that flew around the sky. News media headlined the swamp gas story and for months afterwards cartoonists had a field day. Cartoons about aliens, Dr. Hynek, and swamp gas bloomed like flowers in the Michigan springtime. One showed aliens demanding: "Take us to the scientist who called us swamp gas."

General skepticism about the swamp gas explanation attracted the attention of certain politicians. One was Gerald Ford, the Republican Minority Leader in the House of Representatives. A lot of the sightings were in his Congressional district. He and a Democratic Congressman from the area wrote a letter to the Air Force asking for an independent study of UFOs.

On April 5, 1966, for the first time, Congressional hearings were held about UFOs. The House Armed Services Committee called Air Force witnesses to explain what they were doing about UFOs. As a result, the Air Force decided to accept the recommendation of the February special panel of scientists. They began looking for a college or university who would investigate sightings and study the problem under a contract from the Air Force Office of Scientific Research.

In October, the Air Force announced that the University of Colorado had accepted the contract. The Director of the project would be Dr. Edward U. Condon, a famous scientist who had previously directed the National Bureau of Standards. Everyone, including Dr. Hynek and NICAP, generally approved of this decision. It looked as if there would finally be a thorough scientific investigation instead of what many people felt was an Air Force "numbers game." UFOs, they felt, were a scientific mystery, not a military problem.

In later months the hopeful feelings faded. Dr. Condon attended meetings of contactees, who seemed to fascinate him, and joked about UFOs. At a scientific meeting in January 1967, with the project barely getting started, Dr. Condon's mind already seemed to be made up. "My attitude right now is that there's nothing to it," he said. The Colorado Project staff began arguing among themselves about what they should do.

The Colorado Project report was reviewed by the National Academy of Sciences before it was made public. The reviewers said it was well done and should be accepted by the Air Force. The final report titled *Scientific Study of Unidentified Flying Objects* was released on January 8, 1969.

In a summary at the beginning of the report Dr. Condon said that nothing of value had been learned from the study of UFOs. He said that further study probably wouldn't advance science, and recommended the Air Force discontinue its program.

The report contains several chapters on the history of UFOs and several on ordinary natural events and technology. The sections on actual case studies cover about 91 cases. Almost one-third of these were not explained. Several of the unexplained cases involved photographs or radar. These included the May 1950 McMinnville, Oregon photographs and the August 1950 Great Falls, Montana movie film.

Reaction to the Condon report was immediate. Most scientists praised it, saying, that it proved what they had always known. Major news media tended to echo this praise. The scientists who had studied UFO reports in more detail sided with the UFO groups. They pointed out that Dr. Condon's conclusions were not supported by the evidence presented in the report. In fact, the high percentage of unexplained cases after supposed thorough scientific study left the door wide open that UFOs could be something important.

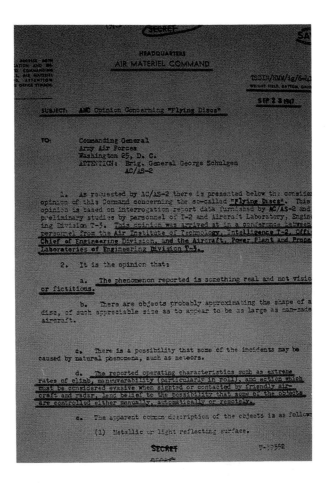

About one year later, in December 1969, the Air Force took Dr. Condon's advice and closed Project Blue Book. Later the Project Blue Book files were put on microfilm and placed in the National Archives in Washington, D.C.

Dr. Condon's report had a lasting impact on Government and scientific studies of UFOs. After 1967 UFO sightings fell off.

For several years after the Condon report UFO sightings did continue, but at a low rate. These were collected by the UFO groups and reported in their newsletters. Since the membership was small, not many people learned about the sightings.

In 1973 Dr. Hynek formed the Center of UFO Studies (CUFOS). This was the second major UFO group to be formed since Project Blue Book was closed. The first was the Mutual UFO Network in May 1969. The Center was formed to serve as a clearinghouse for scientific information about UFOs. The Center also began publication of a journal called the International UFO Reporter. At first there was even a "hotline" number for police departments to call when they received a UFO report.

Late in 1973 the UFOs "struck" again. Just when everyone thought they had "gone away" for good, hundreds – possibly thousands – of people began reporting UFO sightings. Most of the sightings were in September and October.

These and other 1973 sightings reopened the UFO question forcefully. News media once again began asking scientists and other supposed experts whether something unusual really was being seen. People like Dr. Menzel and now Dr. Condon suggested the usual explanations. Furthermore, they now had an "official scientific study" – the Condon report – to "prove" that UFOs do not exist.

The formation of the Center for UFO Studies at this particular time created a lot of interest because Dr. Hynek was a scientist and a former skeptic. Dr. Hynek was careful to point out that he did not know what UFOs were, but that there was a mystery for science to study. Despite his careful approach the news media tended to portray him as a "believer." This hurt his ability to influence scientists.

Because of the 1973 sightings, UFO group memberships increased. The Mutual UFO Network (MUFON) gained investigators throughout the country. They in turn helped to make good UFO reports available. Many of the 1973 sightings were Close Encounters of the Third Kind.

After 1973 the sightings dropped off again. A Gallup poll taken that year showed that almost everyone (95% of the public) was aware of UFOs. Most people (51%) believed they were "real." And many people (11%) have had sightings of things they could not explain.

In December 1977 the movie Close Encounters of the Third Kind was first shown in theaters. It was loosely based on actual UFO sightings. The title was taken from Dr. Hynek's book. He was also a consultant to the movie and appeared for a few seconds at the end in a scene where everyone was standing and watching the landed alien craft.

UFO skeptics predicted that the movie would cause a lot of false sightings. They were wrong. It did cause a slight increase in the number of reports of older sightings by people who were afraid of ridicule, or didn't know where to report a sighting.

Later in 1978 UFO sightings did increase, but more so in Italy and other countries rather than in the U.S. In October a young American pilot, Frederick Valentich, disappeared after reporting a UFO sighting. An object with a green light hovered over his plane. A search failed to locate his body or any wreckage.

During the early morning of December 31, 1978, the crew of a freighter aircraft in New Zealand saw UFOs that were also tracked on radar at times. A news crew on board the plane saw and photographed unexplainable objects. These sightings made international news, and were reported by Walter Cronkite on CBS-TV.

In December 1980 two women and a boy in an automobile driving along a road 35 miles north of Houston, Texas, saw a UFO. A brightly lighted diamond-shaped object hovering over the road

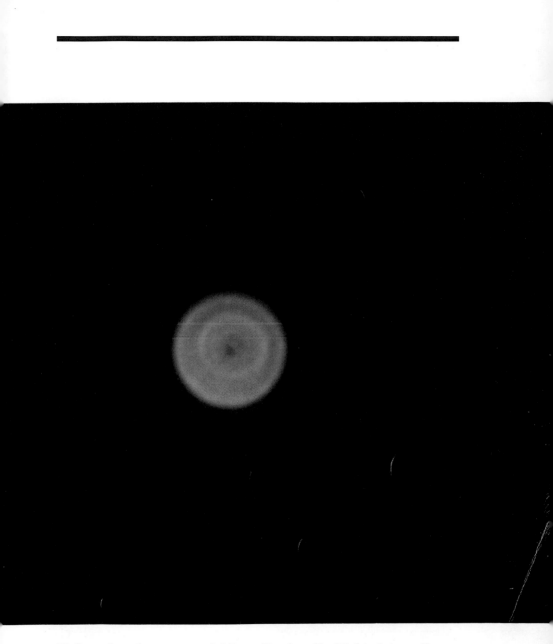

Taken by the crew of New Zealand's Television One
on Clarence River, Kaikoura Coast, on the afternoon
of January 3, 1979.

forced them to stop the car. It was spewing flame down onto the road ahead of them. All three felt uncomfortable heat and experienced burns and radiation poisoning. Then they saw a large number of helicopters flying over the area as if trying to force the UFO to land.

In 1983 and 1984 a large number of people in Westchester County, New York, and in western Connecticut reported UFO sightings. On March 24, 1983, people driving along a highway saw a huge array of lights shaped like a boomerang. It was moving slowly overhead. Many people stopped to look and blocked traffic. Reports of the object poured into police stations and newspaper offices. In July 1984, UFO reports multiplied into the thousands. On July 24 a UFO was filmed on videotape and was seen hovering over a nuclear power plant.

Local UFO investigators held a conference in Brewster, N.Y., in late August of 1984. They rented a 500 seat auditorium. To their surprise, about 1500 people showed up. About 900 of them described UFO sightings to the investigators.

The next UFO sighting to receive major publicity in the U.S. was on November 16, 1986 in Alaska. A Japanese Airlines crew flying a Boeing 747 freighter from Iceland to Japan via Alaska, saw two UFOs almost directly in front of them. A third object apparently was seen off to the right.

The Federal Aviation Administration released a large file of information on this case in March 1987.

In December 1987 *Omni* magazine published a long article about abduction cases. Are they real or imaginary?

With the article was a questionnaire asking about two dozen questions about UFO sightings. It asked what people felt about UFOs and abduction cases in particular. Some of the questions were designed to try to discover whether people answering the questionnaire might really have been abducted by aliens.

Omni readers filled out thousands of these questionnaires. Many of them included letters with the questionnaire. The Fund for UFO

Research in Washington, D.C., analyzed more than 200 of the questionnaires. About 75% of the people who filled them out had sighted a UFO, though few had reported them to anybody.

Nearly 90% believed that some UFO reports might have been caused by real spaceships. Also about 90% thought abduction reports might be true. About 16% showed signs of being abducted. The people who sent in the questionnaires ranged from 13 to 76 years old. Most of their UFO sightings had happened between 1965 and 1985.

Late in 1987 an amazing series of sightings began in Gulf Breeze, Florida, a small town near Pensacola. The sightings continued through the spring of 1988 and then continued off and on for another year. The sightings attracted a lot of publicity because the main witness took dozens of photographs and a videotape of the UFOs. He was later found to be an abductee as well. Many others also saw UFOs flying over the area.

Type of humanoid alien beings described in American abduction reports. Illustration by artist Ted Jacobs.

WHAT DO WE REALLY KNOW

by Richard Hall

What was true on the first page of this book is still true on the last page. *We do not know what UFOs are.* But scientists who have been serious and honest in their work have found out many things about them:

UFOs *do* exist.
UFOs are *not* all nonsense and silliness.
UFOs are seen all over the world.
UFOs are seen by many highly credible people.

Many UFOs look like solid objects. Some look like they are made of metal. Some reflect sunlight. Some have windows and lights on them.

Other UFOs *look* like solid objects but *do* things solid objects cannot do. They make sharp turns at high speeds. Most of them do not make any noise. They do not seem to have motors or engines. They disappear into thin air.

There are many cases where human-shaped beings have been seen near or *in* UFOs. Some people have reported that they have communicated with the beings. Some people have reported that the beings took them into their UFO.

What does all this mean? If these craft cannot be explained as flying machines produced on earth, then what are they? Who or what are the beings manning them? What is their purpose?

I think that either they are beings from somewhere else in space, or they come from another time or dimension reality that our science does not yet understand. Whatever UFOs are, they certainly are a mystery. I and many others will continue to study them. I hope someday we will know the answers.

Colorpainting of two UFOs over Budapest, Hungary on January 23, 1986 by Hungarian artist and ufologist Gyorgy Barth.